What Time Is It?

Written by DeMar Regier
Illustrated by Liza Woodruff

My First
READER

children's press ®

A Division of Scholastic Inc.
New York Toronto London Auckland Sydney
Mexico City New Delhi Hong Kong
Danbury, Connecticut

Library of Congress Cataloging-in-Publication Data

Regier, DeMar, 1928-
  What time is it? / written by DeMar Regier ; illustrated by Liza Woodruff.
      p. cm. — (My first reader)
  Summary: A child is so excited about her grandfather's upcoming visit that she counts down the hours until
he arrives.
  ISBN 0-516-25180-5 (lib. bdg.)   0-516-25279-8 (pbk.)
  [1. Grandfathers—Fiction. 2. Time—Fiction. 3. Stories in rhyme.] I. Woodruff, Liza, ill. II. Title. III. Series.
  PZ8.3+
  [E]—dc22

                                                                          2004015572

Published in 2005 by Children's Press, an imprint of Scholastic Library Publishing.
Published simultaneously in Canada.
Printed in China.

3 4 5 6 7 8 9 10 R 14 13 12 11 10
                                              62

Note to Parents and Teachers

Once a reader can recognize and identify the 47 words used to tell this story, he or she will be able to successfully read the entire book. These 47 words are repeated throughout the story, so that young readers will be able to recognize the words easily and understand their meaning.

The 47 words used in this book are:

a	doesn't	here	Mom	say
at	driving	he's	mop	some
broom	far	his	more	three
called	five	hour	my	today
cannot	flowers	I	needs	two
car	front	I'll	now	wait
clean	gate	is	o'clock	what
coming	Grandpa	it's	one	
Dad	have	just	pick	
did	he	live	room	

Grandpa just called!

What did he say?

Grandpa is coming!

He's coming today!

He's coming at five.

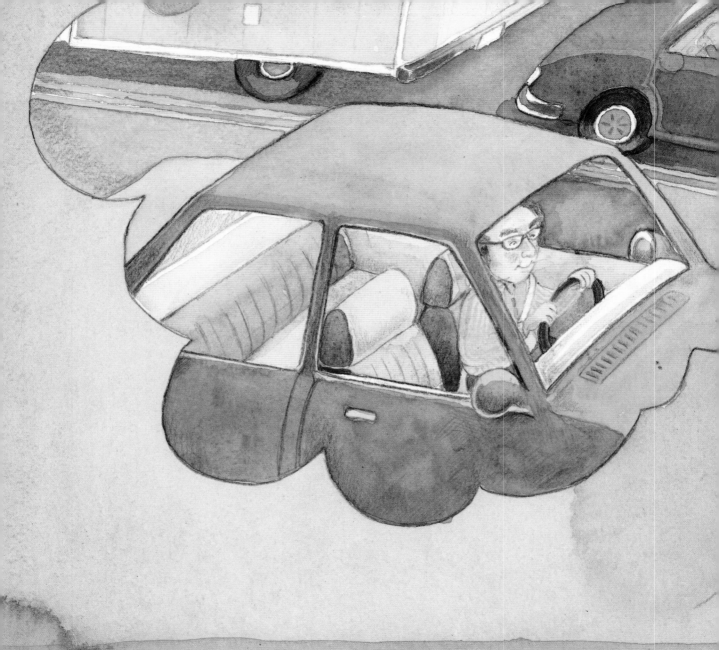

He's driving his car.

It's one o'clock now.

Grandpa doesn't live far!

15

Mom needs a mop.

Dad needs a broom.

It's two o'clock now.

I'll clean my room.

It's three o'clock now.

I'll pick some flowers.

Grandpa is coming!

I have one more hour!

It's five o'clock now.

I cannot wait!

Grandpa is here!

He's at my front gate!

ABOUT THE AUTHOR

DeMar Regier lives in Kansas City where she tends a garden planted for butterflies and birds. There is also a shade area for toads, rabbits, and occasional possums. When she's not writing for children, DeMar enjoys walking her Yorkshire terrier Khory Ires (an anagram for Yorkshire), traveling, listening to jazz, and reading poetry.

ABOUT THE ILLUSTRATOR

Liza Woodruff has always loved both drawing and children, so becoming a children's book illustrator was a dream come true. She has been illustrating books and magazines for more than eight years. Liza lives in rural Vermont with her husband, two children, dog, cats, and, occasionally, chickens!